THE WORLD IS YOURS

OTHER BOOKS BY JIM ROHN

The Seasons of Life

The Five Major Pieces to the Life Puzzle

Twelve Pillars (with Chris Widener)

7 Strategies for Wealth & Happiness

Leading an Inspired Life

The Treasury of Quotes

Excerpts from The Treasury of Quotes

The Jim Rohn Guide to Leadership

The Jim Rohn Guide to Personal Development

The Jim Rohn Guide to Goal Setting

The Jim Rohn Guide to Time Management

The Jim Rohn Guide to Communication

The Jim Rohn One-Year Success Planner

THE WORLD IS YOURS

26 ESSAYS ON LIFE AND SUCCESS

JIM**ROHN**

SUCCESS

Published by SUCCESS Enterprises
750 North St. Paul Street, Suite 250
PMB 30053
Dallas, Texas 75201
www.SUCCESS.com

www.JimRohn.com

SUCCESS® is a registered trademark of SUCCESS Enterprises.
Printed in the United States of America.
10 9 8 7 6 5 4 3

Cover design by Ryan Warren.
Interior design by Megan Knoebel.

"The Time to Act," "Where Do You Go for Your Intellectual Feast?," "Doing the Remarkable," "Achieving Your Dreams," and "Creating Opportunity" were originally published in Jim Rohn's *Leading an Inspired Life*, published by SUCCESS in conjunction with Nightingale-Conant Corporation.

"Establishing Dreams and Goals" and "Leaving a Legacy: Principles to Live By" are from the Jim Rohn One-Year Success Plan, written by Jim Rohn and Chris Widener.

ISBN 978-1-7338313-0-7

SPECIAL SALES
SUCCESS books are available at special discounts for bulk purchase for sales promotions and premiums. Special editions, including personalized covers, excerpts of existing books, and corporate imprints, can be created in large quantities for special needs. For more information, contact Special Markets, SUCCESS, sales@success.com.

"I've traveled the world teaching ideas that count to people who care. It isn't a complex, mystical technique that will require you to undergo some strange form of mental transformation. It is merely a set of basic principles that will get you started on a journey that can be life-changing."

AN INTERNATIONAL TREASURE

For more than 40 years, Jim Rohn honed his craft like a
skilled artist—helping people the world over sculpt life
strategies that expanded their imagination of what is possible.
Those who had the privilege of hearing him speak can attest
to the elegance and common sense of his material. It is no
coincidence, then, that he is still widely regarded as one of the
most influential thinkers of our time, and thought of by many
as an international treasure. He authored countless books
and audio and video programs, and helped motivate and
shape an entire generation of personal-development trainers
and hundreds of executives from America's top corporations.

IDAHO FARM BOY MAKES IT

Born to an Idaho farming family in the mid-1900s, Jim was ingrained with a work ethic that served him well throughout his life. At 25, he met his mentor Earl Shoaff. And over the next six years he made his first fortune, yet didn't get into speaking until he moved to Beverly Hills, Calif., when a friend at the Rotary Club asked him to tell his success story, which Rohn titled "Idaho Farm Boy Makes It to Beverly Hills." His speech went over so well that he received more invitations to share it, and better yet, they started paying him for it. In the beginning, he spoke in front of college and high-school classes and at service clubs, before moving on to seminars in 1963, which launched him into the personal-development business. From then on, he became a trailblazer in the self-help/personal-development industry, impacting the lives of millions through his life-changing material.

HIS INFLUENCE ENDURES

Jim Rohn shared his message with more than 6,000 audiences and over 5 million people all over the world. He received numerous industry awards including the coveted National Speakers Association CPAE Award and the Master of Influence Award. Jim's philosophies and influence continue to have worldwide impact.

Jim focused on the fundamentals of human behavior that most affect personal and business performance. His is the standard to which those who seek to teach and inspire others are compared. He possessed the unique ability to bring extraordinary insights to ordinary principles and events, and the combination of his substance and style still captures the imagination of those who hear or read his words.

For additional information, visit www.JimRohn.com.

CONTENTS

Foreword	11
The Two Choices We Face	17
Change Begins with Choice	23
The Time to Act	29
Nine Things More Important Than Capital	35
Where Do You Go for Your Intellectual Feast?	43
The Power and Value of Attitude	49
Love the Opportunity	55
Success is Easy, But So is Neglect	61
Attitude is Everything	67
Action vs. Self-Delusion	73
Read All the Books	79
What Constitutes a Good Life?	85
Doing the Remarkable	93

CONTENTS

Achieving Your Dreams	99
The Major Key to Your Better Future is You	105
Creating Opportunity	113
Four Words that Make Life Worthwhile	119
Establishing Dreams and Goals	125
Leading a World-Class Life	133
Learn to Deal in Challenges	141
Four Steps to Success	147
Three Key Words to Remember: Weigh, Count and Measure	155
Leaving a Legacy: Principles to Live By	161
The Formula for Failure	167
Learn to Listen to the Right Voice	173
Letting Life Touch Us	179

FOREWORD

Had Jim Rohn been a college professor, there's little doubt his classes would have filled up quickly with a considerable wait list. He might have been a distinguished member of the philosophy, psychology or sociology faculty. Or chairman of the business school. Or even dean of communications and media studies. His expertise and knowledge on a variety of subjects was transcendent.

Perhaps Professor Rohn would have taught courses as diverse as Introduction to Success and Achievement, Essential Principles of Goal Setting, Fundamentals of Productivity and, of course, Obvious 1 and Obvious 2, since Jim often reminded us, "Success is the study of the obvious." Incoming freshmen would have scrambled to sign up for his classes each semester. Upperclassmen would have spoken in reverent tones of the value and practicality of his curriculum.

The fact is that Jim Rohn was, by any measure, a dedicated professor of life studies, but his classroom was not limited to one campus. It extended worldwide. He taught his students in every corner of the globe—in public seminars and private business conferences, via books, audio and video. Young and old soaked in his wisdom and acted on his life-enhancing principles.

Consider this book your introductory text. Intended to be a kind of Jim Rohn primer, it contains a curated compilation of the best of his essays for those seeking life insights. The 26 essays were collected from existing Jim Rohn material, including books and recorded seminars, and make for powerful and valuable reading for new graduates—whether high school or college—and other strivers as they head out in search of success in life.

The title comes directly from one of the featured essays in which Rohn says, "With one dollar and the list I just gave you, **the world is yours**. It belongs to you, whatever piece of it you desire, whatever development you wish for your life."

I can't imagine a more comforting thought for anyone beginning his or her journey toward success. Thank you, Professor Rohn.

Josh Ellis
SUCCESS magazine
Editor-in-Chief

"Like the tree, it would be a worthy challenge for us all to stretch upward and outward to the full measure of our capabilities."

THE TWO CHOICES WE FACE

Each of us has two distinct choices to make about what we will do with our lives. The first choice we can make is to be less than we have the capacity to be: to earn less, to have less, to read less and think less, to try less and discipline ourselves less. These are the choices that lead to an empty life. These are the choices that, once made, lead to a life of constant apprehension instead of a life of wondrous anticipation.

And the second choice? To do it all! To become all that we can possibly be. To read every book that we possibly can. To earn as much as we possibly can. To give and share as much as we possibly can. To strive and produce and accomplish as much as we possibly can. All of us have the choice.

To do or not to do. To be or not to be. To be all or to be less or to be nothing at all.

Like the tree, it would be a worthy challenge for us all to stretch upward and outward to the full measure of our capabilities. Why not do all that we can, every moment that we can, the best that we can, for as long as we can?

Our ultimate life objective should be to create as much as our talent and ability and desire will permit. To settle for doing less than we could do is to fail in this worthiest of undertakings.

Results are the best measurement of human progress. Not conversation. Not explanation. Not justification. Results! And if our results are less than our potential suggests that they should be, then we must strive to become more today than we were the day before. The greatest rewards are always reserved for those who bring great value to themselves and the world around them as a result of whom and what they have become.

"You have the ability to totally transform every area in your life."

CHANGE BEGINS WITH CHOICE

Any day we wish, we can discipline ourselves to change it all. Any day we wish, we can open the book that will open our mind to new knowledge. Any day we wish, we can start a new activity. Any day we wish, we can start the process of life change. We can do it immediately, or next week, or next month, or next year.

We can also do nothing. We can pretend rather than perform. And if the idea of having to change ourselves makes us uncomfortable, we can remain as we are. We can choose rest over labor, entertainment over education, delusion over truth, and doubt over confidence. The choices are ours to make. But while we curse the effect, we continue to nourish the cause. As Shakespeare uniquely observed, "The fault is not in the stars, but in ourselves."

We created our circumstances by our past choices. We have both the ability and the responsibility to make better choices beginning today. Those who are in search of the good life do not need more answers or more time to think things over to reach better conclusions. They need the truth. They need the whole truth. And they need nothing but the truth.

We cannot allow our errors in judgment, repeated every day, to lead us down the wrong path. We must keep coming back to those basics that make the biggest difference in how our life works out. And then we must make the very choices that will bring life, happiness and joy into our daily lives.

And if I may be so bold to offer my last piece of advice for someone seeking and needing to make changes in their life: If you don't like how things are, change it! You're not a tree. You have the ability to totally transform every area in your life. And it all begins with your very own power of choice.

"Discipline enables you to capture the emotion and the wisdom and translate them into action."

THE TIME TO ACT

Engaging in genuine discipline requires that you develop
the ability to take action. You don't need to be hasty if it isn't
required, but you don't want to lose much time either. Here's
the time to act: when the idea is hot and the emotion is strong.

Let's say you would like to build your library. If that is a
strong desire for you, what you've got to do is get the first
book. Then get the second book. Take action as soon as
possible, before the feeling passes and before the idea dims.
If you don't, here's what happens: you fall prey to the law of
diminishing intent.

We intend to take action when the idea strikes us. We intend
to do something when the emotion is high. But if we don't
translate that intention into action fairly soon, the urgency
starts to diminish. A month from now the passion is cold. A
year from now it can't be found.

So take action. Set up a discipline when the emotions are
high and the idea is strong, clear, and powerful. If somebody
talks about good health and you're motivated by it, you
need to get a book on nutrition. Get the book before the idea

passes, before the emotion gets cold. Begin the process. Fall on the floor and do some push-ups. You've got to take action, otherwise the wisdom is wasted. The emotion soon passes unless you apply it to a disciplined activity. Discipline enables you to capture the emotion and the wisdom and translate them into action. The key is to increase your motivation by quickly setting up the disciplines. By doing so, you've started a whole new life process.

Here is the greatest value of discipline: self-worth, also known as self-esteem. Many people who are teaching self-esteem these days don't connect it to discipline. But once we sense the least lack of discipline within ourselves, it starts to erode our psyche. One of the greatest temptations is to just ease up a little bit. Instead of doing your best, you allow yourself to do just a little less than your best. Sure enough, you've started in the slightest way to decrease your sense of self-worth.

There is a problem with even a little bit of neglect. Neglect starts as an infection. If you don't take care of it, it becomes a disease. And one neglect leads to another. Worst of all, when neglect starts, it diminishes our self-worth.

Once this has happened, how can you regain your self-respect? All you have to do is act now! Start with the smallest discipline that corresponds to your own philosophy. Make the commitment: "I will discipline myself to achieve my goals so that in the years ahead I can celebrate my successes."

"What's ingenuity worth?
A fortune. It is more
valuable than money. All
you need is one dollar and
plenty of ingenuity."

NINE THINGS MORE IMPORTANT THAN CAPITAL

When starting any enterprise or business, whether it is full-time or part-time, we all know the value of having plenty of capital (money). But I bet we both know or at least have heard of people who started with no capital and went on to make fortunes. "How?" you may ask.

Well, I believe there are actually some things that are more valuable than capital that can lead to your entrepreneurial success. Let me give you the list.

TIME

Time is more valuable than capital. The time you set aside not to be wasted, not to be given away. Time you set aside to be invested in an enterprise that brings value to the marketplace with the hope of making a profit. Now we have capital time.

How valuable is time? Time properly invested is worth a fortune. Time wasted can be devastation. Time invested can perform miracles, so you invest your time.

DESPERATION

I have a friend, Lydia, whose first major investment in her new enterprise was desperation. She said, "My kids are hungry, I've gotta make this work. If this doesn't work, what will I do?" So she invested $1 in her enterprise selling a product she believed in. The $1 was to buy a few flyers so she could make a sale at retail, collect the money and then buy the product wholesale to deliver back to the customer.

My friend Bill Bailey went to Chicago as a teenager after he got out of high school. And the first job he got was as a night janitor. Someone said, "Bill, why would you settle for night janitor?" He said, "Malnutrition." You work at whatever you can possibly get when you get hungry. You go to work somewhere—night janitor, it doesn't matter where it is. Years later now, Bill is a recipient of the Horatio Alger award, rich and powerful and one of the great examples of lifestyle that I know. But, his first job—night janitor. Desperation can be a powerful incentive. When you say, "I must."

DETERMINATION

Determination says I will. First Lydia said, "I must find a customer." Desperation. Second, she said, "I will find someone before this first day is over." Sure enough, she found someone. She said, "If it works once, it will work again." But then the next person said, "No." Now what must you invest?

COURAGE

Courage is more valuable than capital. If you've only got $1 and a lot of courage, I'm telling you, you've got a good future ahead of you. Courage in spite of the circumstances. Humans can do the most incredible things no matter what happens. Haven't we heard the stories? There are some recent ones from Kosovo that are some of the most classic, unbelievable stories of being in the depths of hell and finally making it out. It's humans. You can't sell humans short. Courage in spite of, not because of, but in spite of. Now once Lydia has made three or four sales and gotten going, here's what now takes over.

AMBITION

"Wow! If I can sell three, I can sell 33. If I can sell 33, I can sell 103." Wow. Lydia is now dazzled by her own dreams of the future.

FAITH

Now she begins to believe she's got a good product. This is probably a good company. And she then starts to believe in herself. Lydia, single mother, two kids, no job. "My gosh, I'm going to pull it off!" Her self-esteem starts to soar. These are investments that are unmatched. Money can't touch it. What if you had a million dollars and no faith? You'd be poor. You wouldn't be rich. Now here is the next one, the reason why she's a millionaire today.

INGENUITY

Putting your brains to work. Probably up until now, you've put about one-tenth of your brainpower to work. What if you employed the other nine-tenths? You can't believe what can happen. Humans can come up with the most intriguing things to do. Ingenuity. What's ingenuity worth? A fortune. It is more valuable than money. All you need is one dollar and plenty of ingenuity. Figuring out a way to make it work, make it work, make it work.

HEART AND SOUL

What is a substitute for heart and soul? It's not money. Money can't buy heart and soul. Heart and soul is more valuable than a million dollars. A million dollars without heart and soul, you have no life. You are ineffective. But, heart and soul is like the unseen magic that moves people, moves people to buy, moves people to make decisions, moves people to act, moves people to respond.

PERSONALITY

You've just got to spruce up and sharpen up your own personality. You've got plenty of personality. Just get it developed to where it is effective every day, effective no matter who you talk to, whether it is a child or whether it is a business person, whether it is a rich person or a poor person. A unique personality that is at home anywhere. One of my mentors, Bill Bailey, taught me, "You've got to learn to be just as comfortable, Mr. Rohn, whether it is in a little shack in Kentucky having a beer and watching the fights with Winfred, my old friend, or in a Georgian mansion in Washington, D.C., as the Senator's guest." Move with ease whether it is with the rich or whether it is with the poor. And it makes no difference to you who is rich or who is poor. A chance to have a unique relationship with whomever. The kind of personality that's comfortable. The kind of personality that's not bent out of shape.

And, lastly, let's not forget charisma and sophistication. Charisma with a touch of humility. This entire list is more valuable than money. With one dollar and the list I just gave you, the world is yours. It belongs to you, whatever piece of it you desire, whatever development you wish for your life. I've given you the secret. Capital. The kind of capital that is more valuable than money and that can secure your future and fortune. Remember that you lack not the resources.

"Feed your mind just as you do your body. Feed it with good ideas, wherever they can be found."

WHERE DO YOU GO FOR YOUR INTELLECTUAL FEAST?

Pity the man who has a favorite restaurant, but not a favorite author. He's picked out a favorite place to feed his body, but he doesn't have a favorite place to feed his mind!

Why would this be? Have you heard about the accelerated learning curve? From birth up until the time we are about eighteen, our learning curve is dramatic, and our capacity to learn during this period is just staggering. We learn a tremendous amount very fast. We learn language, culture, history, science, mathematics... everything!

For some people, the accelerated learning process will continue on. But for most, it levels off when they get their first job. If there are no more exams to take, if there's no demand to get out paper and pencil, why read any more books? Of course, you will learn some things through experience. Just getting out there—sometimes doing it wrong and sometimes doing it right—you will learn.

Can you imagine what would happen if you kept up an accelerated learning curve all the rest of your life? Can you imagine what you could learn to do, the skills you could develop, the capacities you could have? Here's what I'm asking you to do: be that unusual person who keeps up his learning curve and develops an appetite for always trying to find good ideas.

One way to feed your mind and educate your philosophy is through the writings of influential people. Maybe you can't meet the person, but you can read his or her books. Churchill is gone, but we still have his books. Aristotle is gone, but we still have his ideas. Search libraries for books and programs. Search magazines. Search documentaries. They are full of opportunities for intellectual feasting.

In addition to reading and listening, you also need a chance to do some talking and sharing. I have some people in my life who help me with important life questions, who assist me in refining my own philosophy, weighing my values and pondering questions about success and lifestyle.

We all need association with people of substance to provide influence concerning major issues such as society, money, enterprise, family, government, love, friendship, culture, taste, opportunity, and community. Philosophy is mostly influenced by ideas, ideas are mostly influenced by education, and education is mostly influenced by the people with whom we associate.

One of the great fortunes of my life was to be around my mentor, Mr. Shoaff, for five years. During that time he shared with me at dinner, during airline flights, at business conferences, in private conversations and in groups. He gave me many ideas that enabled me to make small daily adjustments in my philosophy and activities. Those daily changes, some very slight, but very important, soon added up to weighty sums.

A big part of the lesson was having Mr. Shoaff repeat the ideas over and over. You just can't hear the fundamentals of life philosophy too often. They are the greatest form of nutrition, the building blocks for a well-developed mind.

I'm asking that you feed your mind just as you do your body. Feed it with good ideas, wherever they can be found. Always be on the lookout for a good idea—a business idea, a product idea, a service idea, an idea for personal improvement. Every new idea will help to refine your philosophy. Your philosophy will guide your life, and your life will unfold with distinction and pleasure.

"A major challenge faced by us all is that we must learn to experience the changing of life's cycles without being changed by them."

THE POWER AND VALUE OF ATTITUDE

Life is about constant, predictable patterns of change. For the six thousand years of recorded history, as humans have entered this world, received parental instruction, classroom instruction, and gathered the experience of life, many have set for themselves ambitious goals, and dreamed lofty dreams. As the wheel of life continues its constant turning, all human emotions appear, disappear, and appear once again.

As we approach the future, for all of us, the only constant factor in life is our feelings and attitudes toward life. A major challenge faced by us all is that we must learn to experience the changing of life's cycles without being changed by them; to make a constant and conscious effort to improve ourselves in the face of changing circumstances.

That is why I believe in the power and value of attitude. As I read, ponder and speculate about people, their deeds and their destiny, I become more deeply convinced that it is our natural destiny to grow, to succeed, to prosper, and to find happiness while we are here. But, it does take effort to continue when our results, as well as our friends, tell us to give up trying. It does not, however, take effort to fail. It requires little more than a slowly deteriorating attitude about our present, our future, and about ourselves. It is ironic that one of the few things in this life that we have total control over is our own attitudes, and yet most of us live our entire life behaving as though we had no control whatsoever.

By our attitude, we decide to read, or not to read. By our attitude, we decide to try or give up. By our attitude, we blame ourselves for our failure, or we blame others. Our attitude determines whether we tell the truth or lie, act or procrastinate, advance or recede, and by our own attitude we and we alone actually decide whether to succeed or fail.

How incredibly unique that a God who would create the complex and immense universe would create the human race and give to those humans the free choice that would permit them to select their own achievement or their own destruction.

This strange, but all-knowing God gave to us a delicately balanced sphere called earth. On it, he placed the intelligent human who would either develop it or destroy it. How terribly fascinating that a God would leave both projects—earth as well as humans—unfinished! Across the rivers and streams He built no bridges. He left the pictures unpainted, the songs unsung, the books unwritten, and space unexplored. For the accomplishment of those things, God created the unfinished human who, within his heart and mind, had the capacity to do all these things and more, depending upon his own choice.

Attitude determines choice, and choice determines results. All that we are, and all that we can become has indeed been left unto us. For as long as you continue to draw breath, you have the chance to complete the work in and for the earth and for yourself that God has begun for you. In the cycles and seasons of life, attitude is everything!

"If you will embrace the disciplines associated with new opportunity, you will soon find that your self-confidence starts to grow."

LOVE THE OPPORTUNITY

Somebody said you have to love what you do, but that's not necessarily true. What is true is that you have to love the opportunity. The opportunity to build life, future, health, success and fortune. Knocking on someone's door or making that extra call may not be something you love to do, but you love the opportunity of what might be behind that door or call.

For example, a guy says, "I'm digging ditches. Should I love digging ditches?" The answer is, "No, you don't have to love digging ditches, but if it is your first entry onto the ladder of success, you say, 'I'm glad somebody gave me the opportunity to dig ditches and I'm going to do it so well, I won't be here long.' "

You can be inspired by having found something, even though you are making mistakes in the beginning and even though it is a little distasteful taking on a new discipline that you haven't learned before. You don't have to love it, you just have to learn to appreciate where you live, appreciate opportunity and appreciate the person who brought you the good news, that found you.

Appreciate the person who believed in you before you believed in yourself. Appreciate the person who said, "Hey, if I can do it, you can do it."

If you will embrace the disciplines associated with the new opportunity, you will soon find that your self-confidence starts to grow, that you go from being a skeptic to being a believer. And soon when you go out person-to-person, talking to people, you will find it to be the most thrilling opportunity in the world. Every person you meet—what could it be? Unlimited! Maybe a friend for life. The next person could be an open door to retiring. The next person could be a colleague for years to come. It's big-time stuff. And sometimes in the beginning, when we are just getting started, we don't always see how big it is.

So, before you are tempted to give up or get discouraged, remember all success is based on long-term commitment, faith, discipline, attitude and a few stepping stones along the way. You might not like the stone you are on right now, but it's sure to be one of the stones that lead to great opportunities in the future.

"Do not neglect to do the simple, basic, 'easy,' but potentially life-changing, activities and disciplines."

SUCCESS IS EASY, BUT SO IS NEGLECT

People often ask me how I became successful in a six-year period while many of the people I knew did not. The answer is simple: The things I found to be easy to do, they found to be easy not to do.

I found it easy to set the goals that could change my life. They found it easy not to. I found it easy to read the books that could affect my thinking and my ideas. They found that easy not to. I found it easy to attend the classes and the seminars, and to get around other successful people. They said it probably really wouldn't matter. If I had to sum it up, I would say what I found to be easy to do, they found to be easy not to do. Six years later, I'm a millionaire and they are all still blaming the economy, the government, and company policies, yet they neglected to do the basic, easy things.

In fact, the primary reason most people are not doing as well as they could and should can be summed up in a single word: neglect.

It is not the lack of money—banks are full of money. It is not the lack of opportunity—America, and much of the free world, continues to offer the most unprecedented and abundant opportunities in the last six thousand years of recorded history. It is not the lack of books—libraries are full of books and they are free! It is not the schools—the classrooms are full of good teachers. We have plenty of ministers, leaders, counselors and advisors.

Everything we would ever need to become rich and powerful and sophisticated is within our reach. The major reason that so few take advantage of all that we have is simply neglect.

Neglect is like an infection. Left unchecked it will spread throughout our entire system of disciplines and eventually lead to a complete breakdown of a potentially joy-filled and prosperous human life.

Not doing the things we know we should do causes us to feel guilty and guilt leads to an erosion of self-confidence. As our self-confidence diminishes, so does the level of our activity. And as our activity diminishes, our results inevitably decline. And as our results suffer, our attitude begins to weaken. And as our attitude begins the slow shift from positive to negative, our self-confidence diminishes even more... and on and on it goes.

So my suggestion is that when given the choice of "easy to" and "easy not to" that you do not neglect to do the simple, basic, "easy," but potentially life-changing, activities and disciplines.

"Our attitude is an asset, a treasure of great value, which must be protected accordingly."

ATTITUDE IS EVERYTHING

The process of human change begins within us. We all have tremendous potential. We all desire good results from our efforts. Most of us are willing to work hard and to pay the price that success and happiness demand.

Each of us has the ability to put our unique human potential into action and to acquire a desired result. But the one thing that determines the level of our potential, that produces the intensity of our activity and predicts the quality of the result we receive is our attitude.

Attitude determines how much of the future we are allowed to see. It decides the size of our dreams and influences our determination when we are faced with new challenges. No other person on earth has dominion over our attitude. People can affect our attitude by teaching us poor thinking habits or unintentionally misinforming us or providing us with negative sources of influence, but no one can control our attitude unless we voluntarily surrender that control.

No one else "makes us angry." We make ourselves angry when we surrender control of our attitude. What someone else may have done is irrelevant. We choose, not they. They merely put our attitude to a test. If we select a volatile attitude by becoming hostile, angry, jealous or suspicious, then we have failed the test. If we condemn ourselves by believing that we are unworthy, then again, we have failed the test.

If we care at all about ourselves, then we must accept full responsibility for our own feelings. We must learn to guard against those feelings that have the capacity to lead our attitude down the wrong path and to strengthen those feelings that can lead us confidently into a better future.

If we want to receive the rewards the future holds in trust for us, then we must exercise the most important choice given to us as members of the human race by maintaining total dominion over our attitude. Our attitude is an asset, a treasure of great value, which must be protected accordingly. Beware of the vandals and thieves among us who would injure our positive attitude or seek to steal it away.

Having the right attitude is one of the basics that success requires. The combination of a sound personal philosophy and a positive attitude about ourselves and the world around us gives us an inner strength and a firm resolve that influences all the other areas of our existence.

"The whole world loves
to watch those who
make things happen."

ACTION VS. SELF-DELUSION

Knowledge fueled by emotion equals action. Action is the ingredient that ensures results. Only action can cause reaction. Further, only positive action can cause positive reaction.

The whole world loves to watch those who make things happen, and it rewards them for causing waves of productive enterprise.

I stress this because today I see many people who are really sold on affirmations. And yet there is a famous saying that "Faith without action serves no useful purpose." How true!

I have nothing against affirmations as a tool to create action. Repeated to reinforce a disciplined plan, affirmations can help create wonderful results.

But there is also a very thin line between faith and folly. You see, affirmations without action can be the beginning of self-delusion—and for your well-being there is little worse than self-delusion.

The man who dreams of wealth and yet walks daily toward certain financial disaster and the woman who wishes for happiness and yet thinks thoughts and commits acts that lead her toward certain despair are both victims of the false hope which affirmations without action can manufacture. Why? Because words soothe and, like a narcotic, they lull us into a state of complacency. Remember this: to make progress you must actually get started!

The key is to take a step today. Whatever the project, start today. Start clearing out a drawer of your newly organized desk... today. Start setting your first goal... today. Start listening to motivational programs... today. Start a sensible weight-reduction plan... today. Start calling on one tough customer a day... today. Start putting money in your new "investment for fortune" account... today. Write a long-overdue letter... today. Anyone can! Even an uninspired person can start reading inspiring books.

Get some momentum going on your new commitment for the good life. See how many activities you can pile on your new commitment to the better life. Go all out! Break away from the downward pull of gravity. Start your thrusters going. Prove to yourself that the waiting is over and the hoping is past—that faith and action have now taken charge.

It's a new day, a new beginning for your new life. With discipline you will be amazed at how much progress you'll be able to make. What have you got to lose except the guilt and fear of the past?

Now, I offer you this challenge: See how many things you can start and continue in this, the first day of your new beginning.

"There is very little difference between someone who cannot read and someone who will not read. The result of either is ignorance."

READ ALL THE BOOKS

All of the books that we will ever need to make us as rich, as healthy, as happy, as powerful, as sophisticated and as successful as we want to be have already been written.

People from all walks of life, people with some of the most incredible life experiences, people that have gone from pennies to fortune and from failure to success have taken the time to write down their experiences so that we might share in their wealth of knowledge. They have offered their wisdom and experience so that we can be inspired by it and instructed by it, and so that we can amend our philosophy by it. Their contributions enable us to reset our sail based upon their experiences. They have handed us the gift of their insights so that we can change our plans, if need be, in order to avoid their errors. We can rearrange our lives based on their wise advice.

All of the insights that we might ever need have already been captured by others in books. The important question is this: In the last ninety days, with this treasure of information that could change our lives, our fortunes, our relationships, our health, our children and our careers for the better, how many books have we read?

Why do we neglect to read the books that can change our lives? Why do we complain but remain the same? Why do so many of us curse the effect but nourish the cause? How do we explain the fact that only a small percent of our entire national population possess and utilize a library card—a card that would give us access to all of the answers to success and happiness we could ever want? Those who wish for the better life cannot permit themselves to miss the books that could have a major impact on how their lives turn out. The book they miss will not help!

And the issue is not that books are too expensive! If a person concludes that the price of buying the book is too great, wait until he must pay the price for not buying it. Wait until he receives the bill for continued and prolonged ignorance.

There is very little difference between someone who cannot read and someone who will not read. The result of either is ignorance. Those who are serious seekers of personal development must remove the self-imposed limitations they have placed on their reading skills and their reading habits. There is a multitude of classes being taught on how to be a good reader and there are thousands of books on the shelves of the public libraries just waiting to be read. Reading is essential for those who seek to rise above the ordinary. We must not permit anything to stand between us and the book that could change our lives.

A little reading each day will result in a wealth of valuable information in a very short time. But if we fail to set aside the time, if we fail to pick up the book, if we fail to exercise the discipline, then ignorance will quickly move in to fill the void.

Those who seek a better life must first become a better person. They must continually seek after self-mastery for the purpose of developing a balanced philosophy of life, and then live in accordance with the dictates of that philosophy. The habit of reading is a major stepping stone in the development of a sound philosophical foundation. And in my opinion, it is one of the fundamentals required for the attainment of success and happiness.

"Friendship is probably
the greatest support
system in the world."

WHAT CONSTITUTES A GOOD LIFE?

The ultimate expression of life is not a paycheck. The ultimate expression of life is not a Mercedes. The ultimate expression of life is not a million dollars or a bank account or a home. Here's the ultimate expression of life in my opinion: living the good life. Here's what we must ask constantly: "What for me would be a good life?" And you have to keep going over and over the list, a list including areas such as spirituality, economics, health, relationships and recreation. What would constitute a good life? I've got a short list.

PRODUCTIVITY

You won't be happy if you don't produce. The game of life is not rest. We must rest, but only long enough to gather strength to get back to productivity. What's the reason for the seasons and the seeds, the soil and the sunshine, the rain and the miracle of life? It's to see what you can do with it, to try your hand. Other people have tried their hand. Now, you try your hand to see what you can do. So part of life is productivity.

GOOD FRIENDS

Friendship is probably the greatest support system in the world. Don't deny yourself the time to develop this support system. Nothing can match it. It's extraordinary in its benefit. Friends are those wonderful people who know all about you and still like you. A few years ago I lost one of my dearest friends. He died at age 53 of a heart attack. David is gone, but he was one of my very special friends. I used to say of David that if I was stuck in a foreign jail somewhere accused unduly and if they would allow me one phone call, I would call David. Why? He would come and get me. That's a friend—somebody who would come and get you. Now we've all got casual friends. And if you called them, they would say, "Hey, if you get back, call me and we'll have a party." So you've got to have both, real friends and casual friends.

CULTURE

Your language, your music, the ceremonies, the traditions, the dress. All of that is so vitally important that you must keep it alive. In fact, it is the uniqueness of all of us that when blended together brings vitality, energy, power, influence, uniqueness and rightness to the world.

SPIRITUALITY

It helps to form the foundation of the family that builds the nation. And make sure you study, practice and teach. Don't be careless about the spiritual part of your nature; it's what makes us who we are, different from animal, dogs, cats, birds and mice. Spirituality.

DON'T MISS ANYTHING

This is what my parents taught me. Don't miss the game. Don't miss the performance, don't miss the movie, don't miss the show, don't miss the dance. Go to everything you possibly can. Buy a ticket to everything you possibly can. Go see everything and experience all you possibly can. This has served me so well to this day. Just before my father died at age 93 if you were to call him at 10:30 or 11:00 at night, he wouldn't be home. He was at the rodeo, he was watching the kids play softball, he was listening to the concert, he was at church, he was somewhere every night.

Live a vital life. Here's one of the reasons why. If you live well, you will earn well. If you live well it will show in your face, it will show in the texture of your voice. There will be something unique and magical about you if you live well. It will infuse not only your personal life but also your business life. And it will give you a vitality nothing else can give.

FAMILY AND THE INNER CIRCLE

Invest in them and they'll invest in you. Inspire them and they'll inspire you. With your inner circle, take care of the details. When my father was still alive, I used to call him when I traveled. He'd have breakfast most every morning with the farmers. Little place called The Decoy Inn out in the country where we lived in Southwest Idaho. So Papa would go there and have breakfast and I'd call him just to give him a special day. Now, if I was in Israel, I'd have to get up in the middle of the night, but it only took five or ten minutes. So I'd call Papa and they'd bring him the phone. I'd say, "Papa I'm in Israel." He'd say, "Israel! Son, how are things in Israel?" He'd talk real loud so everybody could hear—my son's calling me from Israel. I'd say, "Papa last night they gave me a reception on the rooftop underneath the stars overlooking the Mediterranean." He'd say, "Son, a reception on the rooftop underneath the stars overlooking the Mediterranean." Now everybody knows the story. It only took 5 or 10 minutes, but what a special day for my father, age 93.

If a father walks out of the house and he can still feel his daughter's kiss on his face all day, he's a powerful man. If a husband walks out of the house and he can still feel the imprint of his wife's arms around his body, he's invincible all day. It's the special stuff with the inner circle that makes you strong and powerful and influential. So don't miss that opportunity. Here's the greatest value. The prophet said, "There are many virtues and values, but here's the greatest, one person caring for another." There is no greater value than love. Better to live in a tent on the beach with someone you love than to live in a mansion by yourself. One person caring for another, that's one of life's greatest expressions.

So make sure in your busy day to remember the true purpose and the reasons you do what you do. May you truly live the kind of life that will bring the fruit and rewards that you desire.

"Humans can turn nothing into something, pennies into fortune, and disaster into success."

DOING THE REMARKABLE

When it comes to meeting and conquering the negativity in your life, here is a key question: what can you do, starting today, that will make a difference? What can you do during economic chaos? What can you do when everything has gone wrong? What can you do when you've run out of money, when you don't feel well and it's all gone sour? What can you do?

Let me give you the broad answer first. You can do the most remarkable things, no matter what happens. People can do incredible things, unbelievable things, despite the most impossible or disastrous circumstances.

Here is why humans can do remarkable things: because they are remarkable. Humans are different than any other creation. When a dog starts with weeds, he winds up with weeds. And the reason is because he's a dog. But that's not true with human beings. Humans can turn weeds into gardens.

Humans can turn nothing into something, pennies into fortune, and disaster into success. And the reason they can do such remarkable things is because they are remarkable. Try reaching down inside of yourself; you'll come up with some more of those remarkable human gifts. They're there, waiting to be discovered and employed.

With those gifts, you can change anything for yourself that you wish to change. And I challenge you to do that because you can change. If you don't like how something is going for you, change it. If something isn't enough, change it. If something doesn't suit you, change it. If something doesn't please you, change it. You don't ever have to be the same after today. If you don't like your present address, change it—you're not a tree!

If there is one thing to get excited about, it's your ability to make yourself do the necessary things to get a desired result, to turn the negative into success. That's true excitement.

"When you allow your dreams to pull you, they unleash a creative force that can overpower any obstacle in your path."

ACHIEVING YOUR DREAMS

While most people spend most of their lives struggling to earn a living, a much smaller number seem to have everything going their way. Instead of just earning a living, the smaller group is busily working at building and enjoying a fortune. Everything just seems to work out for them. And here sits the much larger group, wondering how life can be so unfair, so complicated and unjust. What's the major difference between the little group with so much and the larger group with so little?

Despite all of the factors that affect our lives—like the kind of parents we have, the schools we attended, the part of the country we grew up in—none has as much potential power for affecting our futures as our ability to dream.

Dreams are a projection of the kind of life you want to lead. Dreams can drive you. Dreams can make you skip over obstacles. When you allow your dreams to pull you, they unleash a creative force that can overpower any obstacle in your path. To unleash this power, though, your dreams must be well defined. A fuzzy future has little pulling power.

Well-defined dreams are not fuzzy. Wishes are fuzzy. To really achieve your dreams, to really have your future plans pull you forward, your dreams must be vivid.

If you've ever hiked a fourteen-thousand-foot peak in the Rocky Mountains, one thought has surely come to mind: How did the settlers of this country do it? How did they get from the East Coast to the West Coast? Carrying one day's supply of food and water is hard enough. Can you imagine hauling all of your worldly goods with you... mile after mile, day after day, month after month? These people had big dreams. They had ambition. They didn't focus on the hardship of getting up the mountain.

In their minds, they were already on the other side—their bodies just hadn't gotten them there yet! Despite all of their pains and struggles, all of the births and deaths along the way, those who made it to the other side had a single vision: to reach the land of continuous sunshine and extraordinary wealth; to start over where anything and everything was possible. Their dreams were stronger than the obstacles in their way.

You've got to be a dreamer. You've got to envision the future. You've got to see California while you're climbing fourteen-thousand-foot peaks. You've got to see the finish line while you're running the race. You've got to hear the cheers when you're in the middle of a monster project. And you've got to be willing to put yourself through the paces of doing the uncomfortable until it becomes comfortable. Because that's how you realize your dreams.

"Remember to work harder on yourself than you do on your job."

THE MAJOR KEY TO YOUR BETTER FUTURE IS YOU

Of all the things that can have an effect on your future, I believe personal growth is the greatest.

We can talk about sales growth, profit growth, asset growth, but all of this probably will not happen without personal growth. It's really the open door to it all. In fact, I'd like to have you memorize a most important phrase. Here it is: The major key to your better future is YOU.

Let me repeat that. The major key to your better future is YOU.

Put that someplace you can see it every day, in the bathroom, in the kitchen, at the office, anywhere you can see it every day. The major key to your better future is YOU. Try to remember that every day you live and think about it. The major key is YOU.

Now, there are many things that will help your better future. If you belong to a strong, dynamic, progressive company, that would help. If the company has good products, good services that you are proud of, that would certainly help. If there are good sales aids, that would help. Good training would certainly help. If there is strong leadership, that will certainly help. All of these things will help.

And, of course, if it doesn't storm, that will help. If your car doesn't break down, that will help. If the kids don't get sick, that will help. If the neighbors stay halfway civil, that will help. If your relatives don't bug you, that will help. If it isn't too cold, if it isn't too hot, all these things will help your better future.

And if prices don't go much higher and if taxes don't get much heavier, that will help. And if the economy stays stable, these things will all help. We could go on and on with the list, but remember this, the list of things that I've just covered and many more—all put together—play a minor role in your better future.

The major key to your better future is you. Lock your mind onto that. This is a super-important point to remember. The major key is you.

A friend of mine is often asked, "How do you develop an above-average income?" He replies:

> *"Simple. Become an above-average person. Work on you. Develop an above-average handshake. A lot of people want to be successful, and they don't even work on their handshake. As easy as that would be to*

start, they let it slide. They don't understand. Develop an above-average smile. Develop an above-average excitement. Develop an above-average dedication. Develop an above-average interest in other people. To have more, become more."

Remember to work harder on yourself than you do on your job. For a long time in my life, I didn't have this figured out.

Strangely enough, with two different people in the same company, one may earn an extra $100 a month, and the other may earn an extra $1,000. What could possibly be the difference? If the products were the same, if the training was the same, if they both had the same literature, the same tools. If they both had the same teacher, the same compensation plan, if they both attended the same meetings, why would one person earn the $100 per month and the other person earn the $1,000?

Remember, here is the difference... the difference is personal, inside, not outside, inside.

You see the real difference is inside you. In fact, the difference is you. Someone once said, "The magic is not in the products. The magic is not in the literature. The magic is not in the film. There isn't a magic meeting, but the magic that makes things better is inside you, and personal growth makes this magic work for you."

The magic is in believing. The magic is in daring. The magic is in trying. The real magic is in persevering. The magic is in accepting. It's in working. The magic is in thinking. There is magic in a handshake. There is magic in a smile. There is magic in excitement and determination. There is real magic in compassion and caring and sharing. There is unusual magic in strong feeling and, you see, all that comes from inside, not outside.

So, the difference is inside you. The real difference is you. You are the major key to your better future.

"Do all you can in preparation of what's to come."

CREATING OPPORTUNITY

An enterprising person is one who comes across a pile of scrap metal and sees the making of a wonderful sculpture. An enterprising person is one who drives through an old decrepit part of town and sees a new housing development. An enterprising person is one who sees opportunity in all areas of life.

To be enterprising is to keep your eyes open and your mind active. It's to be skilled enough, confident enough, creative enough and disciplined enough to seize opportunities that present themselves... regardless of the economy.

A person with an enterprising attitude says, "Find out what you can before action is taken." Do your homework. Do the research. Be prepared. Be resourceful. Do all you can in preparation of what's to come.

Enterprising people always see the future in the present. Enterprising people always find a way to take advantage of a situation, not be burdened by it. And enterprising people aren't lazy. They don't wait for opportunities to come to them, they go after the opportunities. Enterprise means always finding a way to keep yourself actively working toward your ambition.

Enterprise is two things. The first is creativity. You need creativity to see what's out there and to shape it to your advantage. You need creativity to look at the world a little differently. You need creativity to take a different approach, to be different.

What goes hand in hand with the creativity of enterprise is the second requirement: the courage to be creative. You need courage to see things differently, courage to go against the crowd, courage to take a different approach, courage to stand alone if you have to, courage to choose activity over inactivity.

And lastly, being enterprising doesn't just relate to the ability to make money. Being enterprising also means feeling good enough about yourself, having enough self-worth, to want to seek advantages and opportunities that will make a difference in your future. And by doing so you will increase your confidence, your courage, your creativity and your self-worth—your enterprising nature.

"Learning from other people's experiences and mistakes is valuable information."

FOUR WORDS THAT MAKE LIFE WORTHWHILE

Over the years, as I've sought out ideas, principles and strategies to life's challenges, I've come across four simple words that can make living worthwhile.

First, life is worthwhile if you *LEARN*. What you don't know will hurt you. You have to have learning to exist, let alone succeed. Life is worthwhile if you learn from your own experiences—negative or positive. We learn to do it right by first sometimes doing it wrong. We call that a positive negative. We also learn from other people's experiences, both positive and negative. I've always said that it is too bad failures don't give seminars. Obviously, we don't want to pay them so they aren't usually touring around giving seminars. But that information would be very valuable. We would learn how someone who had it all then messed it up. Learning from other people's experiences and mistakes is valuable information because we can learn what not to do without the pain of having tried and failed ourselves.

We learn by what we see, so pay attention. We learn by what we hear, so be a good listener. Now I do suggest that you should be a selective listener. Don't just let anybody dump into your mental factory. We learn from what we read, so learn from every source. Learn from lectures. Learn from songs. Learn from sermons. Learn from conversations with people who care. Always keep learning.

Second, life is worthwhile if you *TRY*. You can't just learn. Now you have to try something to see if you can do it. Try to make a difference. Try to make some progress. Try to learn a new skill. Try to learn a new sport. It doesn't mean you can do everything, but there are a lot of things you can do if you just try. Try your best. Give it every effort. Why not go all out?

Third, life is worthwhile if you *STAY*. You have to stay from spring until harvest. If you have signed up for the day or for the game or for the project, see it through. Sometimes calamity comes and then it is worth wrapping it up. And that's the end. But just don't end in the middle. Maybe on the next project you pass, but on this one, if you signed up, see it through.

And lastly, life is worthwhile if you *CARE*. If you care at all, you will get some results. If you care enough, you can get incredible results. Care enough to make a difference. Care enough to turn somebody around. Care enough to start a new enterprise. Care enough to change it all. Care enough to be the highest producer. Care enough to set some records. Care enough to win.

Four powerful little words: learn, try, stay and care. What difference can you make in your life today by putting these words to work?

"Life is too short to not pursue your dreams."

ESTABLISHING DREAMS AND GOALS

One of the amazing things we have been given as humans is the unquenchable desire to have dreams of a better life and the ability to establish goals to live out those dreams.

Think of it: We can look deep within our hearts and dream of a better situation for ourselves and our families. We can dream of better financial lives and better emotional or physical lives. Certainly, we can dream of better spiritual lives.

But what makes this even more powerful is that we have been given the ability to not only dream but to pursue those dreams. And not only pursue them, but the cognitive ability to actually lay out a plan and strategies (setting goals) to achieve those dreams. Powerful!

What are your dreams and goals? This isn't what you already have or what you have done, but what you want. Have you ever really sat down and thought through your life values and decided what you really want? Have you ever taken the time to truly reflect, to listen quietly to your heart, to see what dreams live within you? Your dreams are there. Everyone has them. They may live right on the surface, or they may be buried deep from years of others telling you they were foolish, but they are there.

So how do we know what our dreams are? This is an interesting process and it relates primarily to the art of listening. This is not listening to others. It is listening to yourself. If we listen to others, we hear their plans and dreams—and many will try to put their plans and dreams on us. If we listen to others, we can never be fulfilled. We will only chase elusive dreams that are not rooted deep within us. No, we must listen to our own hearts.

Let's take a look at some practical steps and thoughts on hearing from our hearts about what our dreams are.

Take time to be quiet. This is something that we don't do enough of in this busy world of ours. We rush, rush, rush, and we are constantly listening to noise all around us. The human heart was meant for times of quiet, to peer deep within. It is when we do this that our hearts are set free to soar and take flight on the wings of our own dreams! Schedule some quiet "dream time" this week. No other people. No cellphone. No computer. Just you, a pad, a pen, and your thoughts.

Think about what really thrills you. When you are quiet, think about those things that really get your blood moving. What would you LOVE to do, either for fun or for a living? What would you love to accomplish? What would you try if you were guaranteed to succeed? What big thoughts move your heart into a state of excitement and joy? When you answer these questions, you will feel great and you will be in the "dream zone." It is only when we get to this point that we experience what our dreams are!

Write down all of your dreams as you have them. Don't think of any as too outlandish or foolish—remember, you're dreaming! Let the thoughts fly and take careful record.

Now, prioritize those dreams. Which are most important? Which are most feasible? Which would you love to do the most? Put them in the order in which you will actually try to attain them. Remember, we are always moving toward action, not just dreaming.

Here is the big picture: Life is too short to not pursue your dreams. Someday your life will near its end and all you will be able to do is look backward. You can reflect with joy or regret. Those who dream, who set goals and act on them to live out their dreams, are those who live lives of joy and have a sense of peace when they near the end of their lives. They have finished well, for themselves and for their families.

Remember: These are the dreams and goals that are born out of your heart and mind. These are the goals that are unique to you and come from who you were created to be and gifted to become. Your specific goals are what you want to attain because they are what will make your life joyful and bring your family's life into congruence with what you want it to be.

"Set your goals. Know what you want and how you are going to get there."

LEADING A WORLD-CLASS LIFE

Every four years the world is given the gift of the Olympics. For a few weeks, nations lay down their arms and come together to let their world-class athletes compete on a level playing field to see who the best is in the many events. Such amazing athleticism is on display. It boggles the mind what these young men and women can accomplish with their bodies. Great feats of skill and determination bring them to the pinnacle of athletic achievement. Incredible.

As I think about what it takes to become a world-class athlete capable of competing at the Olympic level, I realize that there are some foundational lessons for all of us to learn as it relates to becoming world class in whatever we set our hands to.

The secret of how these athletes became world class is found in the combination of two fundamental ideas: desire and dedication.

A 22-year-old man doesn't simply wake up one day and find that he is on the Olympic basketball team. No, it started years before. In fact, it probably started when he was only six or seven years old. Maybe his father took him to a basketball game and that little boy said, "Someday, Daddy, I am going to be a basketball player." That was the first sign of desire. Desire is key. World-class people start with desire. They have to at some point "want it."

But we all know people who dream of big things and never accomplish those dreams, don't we? Why is that? After all, they have desire. They want it. But the engine that drives the dream is dedication. Desire tells you what you want, while dedication is what will get it for you.

Someone may see a young gymnast and say, "Wow, that looks easy." What they don't see or perhaps overlook is the years of practice. The years of getting up at 4:30 every morning and going to the gym before going to school. It is the dedication of the young athlete, the many times of failing in practice, the many times of falling off the equipment and faithfully getting back on that turns a wisher into a world-class doer.

A person with desire but no dedication will never achieve much. You must have the powerful combination of both.

So let's take a closer look at each of these and gain some insight into what desire and dedication are all about.

Desire. There are three parts to desire:

- Dreaming
- The Vision
- Focus

First is dreaming. Have you let yourself dream lately? Just sit down and begin to imagine all of the incredible possibilities your life could become? Spend some time just dreaming.

Next is the vision. Once you dream, you begin to cut back on all of the possibilities and narrow down to the possibility that you really want. You begin to create a vision for your life. You begin to see your life as you want it.

Last is focus. Once you have the vision, you have to focus in on that dream. This is where you get specific about what your life is going to look like.

Dedication. There are also three parts to dedication:

- The Plan
- Beginning
- Perseverance

First is the plan. Without a plan, you will drift. You will certainly not carry out your dream if you do not have a plan. Write it down. Set your goals. Know what you want and how you are going to get there.

Second is the beginning. This may sound simple and yet it is simply profound. Many people have a dream and a plan, but they never begin. It's so simple. Just start. The first step on the long journey is still just one step. If you have a dream and a plan, take a step in the right direction.

Last is to persevere. Every road to every dream has a hard-to-travel section or sections. Every great dream will encounter difficulty. The question isn't whether or not you will encounter trouble, but how you will respond to trouble. Will you quit when the going gets tough? Or will you persevere? I have found that every successful person I know, myself included, has encountered problems along the way that tempted them to quit. Yet they persevered and achieved their dream.

Let's take a look at the progression. As you do, think about where you are in the progression of becoming a world-class dream pursuer.

1. Dream
2. Create a vision
3. Focus the vision
4. Develop a plan
5. Begin to pursue the dream
6. Persevere

Friends, I hope for you the fulfillment of every dream that you have. That is what life is about, isn't it? But to do so, I know that you will have to combine your desire with good old dedication. And when you combine those two, you will be well on your way to leading a world-class life!

"A person could do extraordinary things when somebody says, 'Let's.'"

LEARN TO DEAL IN CHALLENGES

If you really want to help people in extraordinary ways, learn to deal in challenges. That is what sports is all about, challenges. That is what music is all about. The challenge to play so well that someone is inspired. The challenge to say it so well that someone gets it. The challenge to be so gifted in language that someone sees it. Insight is unbelievable. Only human beings can do this.

The man closes his eyes and says, "I see it." You say, "No, you don't, you've got your eyes closed." No. There is more than one way to see. All someone has to do is to see an answer that they can start on immediately and within six months their life could start to multiply and change. Within one year, the difference will be extraordinary and a person who was once lost now becomes a person of influence, just because someone helped them to see for the moment what was wrong and the possibility of change. Then they accept the challenge to go do it and do it well.

Now here is the best challenge of all: "Let's go do it." Don't always say, "You go do it, you change," but rather, "Let's get healthy, let's go change the world, let's build an enterprise, let's work on this together."

See, I always respond better to, "Let's." Sometimes it's hard to lift yourself out. It's hard to be self-inspired at first. And then someone says, "Come on, let's start a new program," "Come on, let's do exercises," "Come on, let's get healthy," "Come on, let's start something. I'll be there. You be there. You bring a guest and I'll bring a guest. Let's start something." That is so inspiring to have somebody say, "Let's." Let's do it. Let's build a team. Let's win the championship. Let's walk off with the trophy!

"Let's." Wow. There is something about it that can keep you awake at nights. There is something about it that turns on the juices. There is something about it that reaches deep in the soul. A person could do extraordinary things when somebody says, "Let's." "Let's do it. I've got two with me already if you'll be the next one we can conquer the world." You say, "Whoa. Together nobody is a match for us. By yourself, you're vulnerable; but with us, nobody is a match." You say, "Wow! I want to belong to that team." So figure out ways to say, "Let's."

"Be a collector of good ideas."

FOUR STEPS TO SUCCESS

Let me pass on to you these four simple steps to success:

Number one is good ideas. Be a collector of good ideas. My mentor taught me to keep a journal when I was 25 years old. I've been doing it now all these years. They will be passed on to my children and my grandchildren. If you hear a good health idea, capture it. Write it down. Don't trust your memory.

Then on a cold wintry evening, go back through your journal, the ideas that changed your life, the ideas that saved your marriage, the ideas that bailed you out of bankruptcy, the ideas that helped you become successful, the ideas that made you millions. What a good review. Going back over the collection of ideas that you gathered over the years. So be a collector of good ideas for your business, for your relationships, for your future.

The next step to success is to have good plans. A good plan for the day, a good plan for the future, a good health plan, a good plan for your marriage. Building anything is like building a house. You need to have a plan.

Now here is a good time management question: When should you start the day? Answer: As soon as you have it finished. Building a life is like building a house. What if you just started laying bricks and somebody asks, "What are you building?" And you say, "I have no idea." See? They would come and take you away to a safe place. So, don't start the house until you finish it. Now, is it possible to finish the house before you start it? Yes, but it would be foolish to start before you had it finished. Not a bad time management idea. Don't start the day until it is pretty well finished—at least the outline of the day. Leave some room to improvise. Leave some room for extra strategies, but finish it before you start it.

And here is the next piece that is a little more challenging: Do not start the week until you have it finished. Lay it out, structure it, and then put it to work. Then the next one is a little tougher yet. Do not start the month until you have it finished.

Finally, the big one. Don't start the year until it is finished on paper. It's not a bad idea, toward the end of the year, to sit down with your family for the family-structure plans. Sit down in your business for the business plans. Sit down with your financial advisor for your investments and map out the year, properties to buy, properties to sell, places to go with your family. Lay out the year. I finally learned to do that. It was also helpful for my family to show them where they appeared on my calendar. You know, I used to have my business things on there and I used to have my lectures and my seminars all laid out on my calendar. Guess what the children said? "Where are we on the game plan? Please show us our names on the game plan." So you need to do it for your children, for your spouse, for your friends.

Now, here is the third step to success, and it can be really challenging. Learning to handle the passing of time. It takes time to build a career. It takes time to make changes. So give your project time. Give your people time. If you're working with people, give them time to learn, grow, change, develop, produce. And here is the big one: give yourself time. It takes time to master something new. It takes time to make altered changes and refinement in philosophy as well as activity. Give yourself time to learn, time to get it, time to start some momentum, time to finally achieve. It is easy to be impatient with yourself. I remember when I first tried to learn to tie my shoes. It seemed like it would take me forever. Finally, I got it and it didn't take forever, but it seemed like for a while I'd never learn. I'd get it backward. The bow goes up and down instead of across. How do I straighten that out? Finally I got it. It just took time.

Mama taught me a little bit about playing the piano. "Here is the left-hand scale," she'd say. I got that. It was easy. Then she said, "Here is the right-hand scale." I got that. That was easy. Now she said, "We are going to play both hands at the same time." I said, "Well, how can you do that?" Now one at a time was easy... but at the same time? Looking at this hand and looking at that hand, I finally got it. Finally, I got where I could play the scales with both hands.

Then I remember the day she said, "Now we are going to read the music and play with both hands." I thought, "You can't do all that." But you know, sure enough, I'm looking at the music, looking at each hand, a little confused at first, but finally I mastered it. It took a little time to read the music and play with both hands. Then I remember the day she said, "Now we are going to watch the audience, read the music and play with both hands." I thought, "Now that is going too far!" How could you possibly do that? But adding them one at a time and giving myself time to master one before we went to the next one allowed me to get to where I could watch the audience, read the music and play with both hands. So the lesson here is: Give yourself time. You can become a better pro. You can better master the art of parenting. You can better master the art of managing time, conserving resources, working together as a partner. Give yourself time.

And here's the last one: Learning to solve problems. Business problems, family problems, financial problems, emotional problems—challenges for us all. Here's the best way to treat a problem: As an opportunity to grow. Change if you have to. Modify if you must. Discard an old philosophy that wasn't working well for a new one. The best phrase my mentor ever gave me was when he said, "Mr. Rohn, if you will change, everything will change for you." Wow. I took that to heart, and sure enough the more I changed the more everything changed for me.

So learn to master good ideas, have good plans, handle the passing of time and solve problems and you will be on your way to more success than you could ever imagine!

"Life expects you to make
measurable progress
in reasonable time."

THREE KEY WORDS TO REMEMBER: WEIGH, COUNT AND MEASURE

Here are three key words to remember: weigh, count and measure. Now why weigh, count and measure? To see what your results are from your activity, your attitude and your philosophy. If you find that the results are not to your liking, there are only three places to look. Your philosophy needs to be fine-tuned, your attitude needs to be strengthened, or your disciplines need extra skill. But that's it. Activity, attitude and philosophy create results.

Now, on results I teach that life expects you to make measurable progress in reasonable time. But you must be reasonable with time. You can't say to someone every five minutes, "How are you doing now?" That's too soon to ask for a count. A guy says, "I haven't left the building yet. Give me a break!" You can't wait five years. That's too long. Too many things can go wrong waiting too long for a count to see how you're doing.

Here are some good timeframes:

First, at the end of the day. You can't let more than a day go by without looking at some things and making progress. The New Testament says if you are angry try to solve it before the sun goes down. Don't carry anger for another day. It may be too heavy to carry. If you try to carry it for a week, it may drop you to your knees. So, some things you must get done in a day.

Here's the next timeframe: a week. We ask for an accounting of the week so we can issue the pay. And whatever you've got coming, that's what you get when the week is over. Now in business there are two things to check in the course of the week: your activity count and your productivity count. Because activity leads to productivity, we need to count both to see how we're doing.

My mentor taught me that success is a numbers game, and very early he started asking me my numbers. He asked, "How many books have you read in the last 90 days?" I said, "Zero." He said, "Not a good number." He said, "How many classes have you attended in the last six months to improve your skills?" I said, "Zero." He said, "Not a good number." Then he said, "In the last six years that you've been working, how much money have you saved and invested?" Again, I said, "Zero," and he said, "Not a good number." Then here's what else he said, "Mr. Rohn, if these numbers don't change, your life won't change. But if you'll start improving these numbers, then perhaps you'll start to see everything change for you."

Success and results are a numbers game. John joins this little sales company. He's supposed to make 10 calls the first week just to get acquainted with the territory. So on Friday we call him in and say what? "How many calls?" He says, "Well." You say, "John, 'well' won't fit in the little box here. I need a number." Now he starts with a story. And you say, "John, the reason I made this little box so small is so a story won't fit. All I need is a number because if you give us the number we're so brilliant around here we could guess the story." It's the numbers that count. Making measurable progress in reasonable time.

Here's the best accounting. The accounting you make of yourself. Don't wait for the government to do it, don't wait for the company to do it. But you've got to add up some of your own numbers and ask, "Am I making the progress I want and will it take me where I want to go now and in the future?" You be the judge!

"There is always time to do more and achieve more, to help more and serve more, to teach more and to learn more."

LEAVING A LEGACY: PRINCIPLES TO LIVE BY

You know me. I am a philosopher. I love principles. Yes, actions are great and I talk about them regularly, but the important stuff is what lies underneath—the principles.

Here are what I consider the principles that we must commit to if we are to leave the legacy we desire:

1. Life is best lived in service to others. This doesn't mean that we do not strive for the best for ourselves. It does mean that in all things we serve other people, including our family, co-workers and friends.

2. Consider others' interests as important as your own. Much of the world suffers simply because people consider only their own interests. People are looking out for number one, but the way to leave a legacy is to also look out for others.

3. Love your neighbor even if you don't like him. It is interesting that Jesus told us to love others. But he never tells us to like them. Liking people has to do with emotions.

Loving people has to do with actions. And what you will find is that when you love them and do good by them, you will more often than not begin to like them.

4. Maintain integrity at all costs. There are very few things you take to the grave with you. The number one thing is your reputation and good name. When people remember you, you want them to think, "She was the most honest person I knew. What integrity." There are always going to be temptations to cut corners and break your integrity. Do not do it. Do what is right all of the time, no matter what the cost.

5. You must risk in order to gain. In just about every area of life, you must risk in order to gain the reward. In love, you must risk rejection in order to ask that person out for the first time. In investing, you must place your capital at risk in the market in order to receive the prize of a growing bank account. When we risk, we gain. And when we gain, we have more to leave for others.

6. You reap what you sow. In fact, you always reap more than you sow—you plant a seed and reap a bushel. What you give you get. What you put into the ground then grows out of the ground. If you give love, you will receive love. If you give time, you will gain time. It is one of the truest laws of the universe. Decide what you want out of life and then begin to sow it.

7. Hard work is never a waste. No one will say, "It is too bad he was such a good, hard worker." But if you aren't they will surely say, "It's too bad he was so lazy—he could have been so much more!" Hard work will leave a grand legacy. Give it your all on your trip around the earth. You will do a lot of good and leave a terrific legacy.

8. Don't give up when you fail. Imagine what legacies would have never existed if someone had given up. How many thriving businesses would have been shut down if they quit at their first failure? Everyone fails. It is a fact of life. But those who succeed are those who do not give up when they fail. They keep going and build a successful life—and a legacy.

9. Don't ever stop in your pursuit of a legacy. Many people have accomplished tremendous things later on in life. There is never a time to stop in your pursuit of a legacy. Sometimes older people will say, "I am 65. I'll never change." That won't build a great life! No, there is always time to do more and achieve more, to help more and serve more, to teach more and to learn more. Keep going and growing that legacy!

These are core principles to live by if you want to become the kind of person who leaves a lasting legacy.

"Failure is nothing more than a few errors in judgment repeated every day."

THE FORMULA FOR FAILURE

Failure is not a single, cataclysmic event. We do not fail overnight. Failure is the inevitable result of an accumulation of poor thinking and poor choices. To put it more simply, failure is nothing more than a few errors in judgment repeated every day.

Now why would someone make an error in judgment and then be so foolish as to repeat it every day?

The answer is because he or she does not think that it matters.

On their own, our daily acts do not seem that important. A minor oversight, a poor decision, a wasted hour generally don't result in an instant and measurable impact. More often than not, we escape any immediate consequences of our deeds.

If we have not bothered to read a single book in the past 90 days, this lack of discipline does not seem to have any immediate impact on our lives. And since nothing drastic happened to us after the first 90 days, we repeat this error in judgment for another 90 days, and on and on it goes. Why?

Because it doesn't seem to matter. And herein lies the great danger. Far worse than not reading the books is not even realizing that it matters!

Those who eat too many of the wrong foods are contributing to a future health problem, but the joy of the moment overshadows the consequence of the future. It does not seem to matter. Those who smoke too much or drink too much go on making these poor choices year after year after year... because it doesn't seem to matter. But the pain and regret of these errors in judgment have only been delayed for a future time. Consequences are seldom instant; instead, they accumulate until the inevitable day of reckoning finally arrives and the price must be paid for our poor choices— choices that didn't seem to matter.

Failure's most dangerous attribute is its subtlety. In the short term, those little errors don't seem to make any difference. We do not seem to be failing. In fact, sometimes these accumulated errors in judgment occur throughout a period of great joy and prosperity in our lives. Since nothing terrible happens to us, since there are no instant consequences to capture our attention, we simply drift from one day to the next, repeating the errors, thinking the wrong thoughts, listening to the wrong voices and making the wrong choices. The sky did not fall in on us yesterday; therefore, the act was probably harmless. Since it seemed to have no measurable consequence, it is probably safe to repeat.

But we must become better educated than that!

If, at the end of the day, when we made our first error in judgment the sky had fallen in on us, we undoubtedly would have taken immediate steps to ensure that the act would never be repeated. Like the child who places his hand on a hot burner despite his parents' warnings, we would have had an instantaneous experience accompanying our error in judgment.

Unfortunately, failure does not shout out its warnings as our parents once did. This is why it is imperative to refine our philosophy in order to be able to make better choices. With a powerful personal philosophy guiding our every step, we become more aware of our errors in judgment and more aware that each error really does matter.

"Be ever mindful of the inner urgings that would have us repeating costly errors."

LEARN TO LISTEN TO THE RIGHT VOICE

Why are we so frequently inclined to do the things that are least important but so reluctant to do the essential things that success and happiness demand? What is that voice that whispers to us, "Just let it all slide. Why worry about all that discipline nonsense?" It is the voice of negativity, a voice that has grown increasingly stronger over the years as a result of being around the wrong influences, thinking the wrong thoughts, developing the wrong philosophy and making the wrong decisions.

Part of the solution to quieting the voice of negativity is learning to listen to the still, small voice of success, which resides inside each of us. The voice of success is constantly struggling to be heard above the loud promptings of the voice of failure. Our own free agency allows us to follow whichever voice we choose. Every time we allow ourselves to succumb to the voice of the dark side of life, and are persuaded to repeat errors instead of mastering new disciplines, the voice of negativity grows stronger. Conversely, each time we listen to the urgings of the voice of success and are persuaded to turn off the television and pick up a book, to open our journals and record our thoughts or to spend a quiet moment pondering where our current actions may be leading us, the voice of success responds to these new disciplines and grows in strength and volume as each day passes. For each new discipline, another step forward.

We can never totally eradicate the voice of failure from within us. It will always be there, urging us to think and feel and act in a way that is contrary to our own best interests. But we can effectively silence this destructive influence by developing a sound philosophy and a positive attitude about life and our future.

Creating a new philosophy is easy to do. Making new and better decisions is easy to do. Developing a new attitude is easy to do. All of the worthwhile and rewarding things we desire are easy to do, but the major challenge—the one that could leave us with pennies instead of fortune and trinkets instead of treasures—is that it is also easy not to do.

We must keep a watchful eye on the subtle differences between success and failure, and be ever mindful of the inner urgings that would have us repeating costly errors rather than developing new disciplines.

We must each make our own conscious decision to reach out for the good life through the refinement of our thoughts and the careful examination of the potential consequences of our accumulated errors. We must not allow ourselves to think that the errors do not matter. They do. We must not allow ourselves to assume that a lack of discipline in one small area of our lives will not make a difference. It will. And we must not allow ourselves to believe that we can have all that we want to have and become all that we wish to be without making any changes in the way we think about life. We must.

The journey toward the good life begins with a serious commitment to changing any aspect of our current philosophy that has the capacity to come between us and our dreams. The remaining pieces of the puzzle of life can be of little value if we have not first made the firm resolve to do something with this piece of the puzzle.

Everything is within our reach if we will read the books, use the journals, practice the disciplines, and wage a new and vigorous battle against neglect. These are some of the fundamental activities that lead not only to the development of a new philosophy but to a new life filled with joy and accomplishment. Each new and positive activity weakens the grip of failure and steers us ever closer to the destination of our choice. Each new, disciplined step taken toward success strengthens our philosophical posture and increases our chances of achieving a well-balanced life. But the first step in realizing this worthy achievement lies in becoming the master of our ship and the captain of our soul by developing a sound personal philosophy.

"Only when we have experienced the full spectrum of human existence can we begin to design and live a life of substance."

LETTING LIFE TOUCH US

There is a world of difference between going to Paris and experiencing Paris. Going is a basic physical activity. Experiencing is a rich emotional event.

To experience life, we must let it touch us. And not just the positive experiences. We must also be touched by the sorrows and the sadness, by the losses and the longings. Emotions enrich our lives and create for us a special uniqueness in terms of both who we are and how we live.

To live a unique life we must first become unique individuals by perceiving a broad range of human experiences and emotions. Only when we have experienced the full spectrum of human existence can we begin to design and live a life of substance.

All progress begins with an emotion. We do not attract a better life merely by wanting it; we attract it by adopting the emotions that those with the "better life" possess.

If we want to be happy, we begin by thinking and feeling and acting "happy."

If we want to be wealthy, we begin by thinking and feeling and acting "wealthy."

Any father who wishes can capture the attention and the appreciation of his family with his current resources. He does not have to wait for the wealth in order to discover and share the happiness. He does not have to wait in order to be unique. He does not have to postpone the experience of happiness and a unique lifestyle, because it is within his current reach. In fact, practicing what is within his current reach will actually extend his reach. He only has to start with where he is and with what he has. He needs only to breathe happiness and uniqueness into his current assets.

The joy that could be shared by surprising his daughter with a $20 concert ticket, when that is all he can currently do, can be just as rewarding as giving her a $20,000 automobile. This is especially true if, in the past, he has argued with his daughter about her insistence on wanting to "waste money on such foolishness" as a concert. Imagine the father—the head of the family who wants to be sophisticated and wealthy— crumbling up a $20 bill and throwing it at his daughter as an expression of his disapproval about the concert that is so important to her!

How much better it would be if he were to surprise his daughter one day by going out of his way to purchase the ticket for her in advance, and then presenting it to her in some special manner and with a few special words. How much more meaningful still it would be if the father were to purchase two tickets and attend the concert with his daughter. Perhaps as an added touch he could combine the concert with a private dinner at a special place where the food would be extraordinary and the service unique.

That is what lifestyle is all about: finding unique ways of transforming emotional possibilities into meaningful experiences that are within our current means.

We can start right now by offering all that is within our power to share. Whether we offer our time, a shoulder to cry on, a word of sincere appreciation or our undivided attention, if we will just be there and really live that moment, what an experience that could be!

We must not let the years, and the chances, and the small opportunities for creating moments of joy slip away. If we continue to wait until we have the resources to do the big things before we master the art of experiencing all that life currently has to offer, then we may find that we have waited too long.

Let us begin this very day the process of creating a wealth of experiences and memories that will endure in the hearts of those we love long after we are gone.

Lifestyle is a source of joy and fulfillment that is available to us all, regardless of our current circumstances. It is within the immediate reach of anyone willing to make it a serious study.

Our lives are filled with opportunities for experiencing a new level of happiness and sophistication and appreciation. All that is required is a change of mind and a decision to begin experiencing it all now. And as we demonstrate our new commitment to take full measure from even the smallest opportunities that come our way, life will see to it that far greater experiences than we ever dreamed will soon become our certain reward.

JIM ROHN RESOURCES

Jim Rohn's philosophies and influence continue to have worldwide impact. If you enjoyed this book, consider these popular Jim Rohn books and programs to inspire you to an exceptional life!

THE SEASONS OF LIFE

THE TREASURY OF QUOTES

THE FIVE MAJOR PIECES TO THE LIFE PUZZLE

TWELVE PILLARS
WITH CHRIS WIDENER

THE WEEKEND SEMINAR

LEADING AN INSPIRED LIFE

LIVING AN EXCEPTIONAL LIFE

CHALLENGE TO SUCCEED

To order, go to **store.JimRohn.com** or call **800-929-0434.** While you're there, sign up for the FREE Jim Rohn Weekly Newsletter!

THE JIM ROHN GUIDE SERIES

The timeless wisdom of Jim Rohn in concise, easy-to-read guides. Perfect for sharing with friends, family, business associates, clients and prospects.

TIME MANAGEMENT
PERSONAL DEVELOPMENT
LEADERSHIP
GOAL SETTING
COMMUNICATION

Quantity discounts available

store.JimRohn.com or store.SUCCESS.com